# SUICIDE LETTERS

## MARIA L. DAVILA

**A journey of Faith, Forgiveness, Freedom, and finding purpose in our pain.**

# SUICIDE LETTERS

## MARIA L. DAVILA

Published by:
MODERN DAY DISCIPLE, LLC| FLORIDA

Maria Davila and Modern Day Disciple, LLC titles may be purchased in bulk for educational, business, fundraising, or sales promotional use; for information, please use email her.missions.by.maria@gmail.com

Table of Contents

# Dedication

To every reader holding these pages: thank you for your courage. Thank you for daring to confront your own pain and for trusting me to walk with you through it. This book is not just my story; it is a testament to what God can do in all of us when we choose to surrender over silence.

# Author's Note:

*This book discusses sensitive topics such as trauma, suicidal thoughts, and violation in the context of faith and healing. If you are in crisis, please reach out for help. You are not alone.*

## He Changed Me (written by Maria Davila in 2001)

*I needed changes to be made. The ways I*
*chose to live. Before my priorities fade*
*There was a sacrifice I had to give.*

*My Bibles were my tools. To raise my family*
*on solid ground. I started breaking all the*
*rules. And quicksand is what I found.*

*He gives me strength; He gives me love.*
*Everything I have comes from up above.*
*More than my Mother and my Father, He*
*loves me so much. He handed me a key with*
*His heavenly touch.*

*Yet, I'd still drink and I'd still smoke.*
*Didn't think about the words He spoke.*
*He loved me so much, He took every whip.*
*Why did I continue to take a sip?*

*We will hide from the sins that we have*
*done. But Jesus stood up and died for each*
*and every one. He cleansed me, forgave me,*
*and washed away my sin. He pulled me out*
*from the pit of Hell I fell in*

*Oh Lord, forgive me, for all I've done. All of*
*those things are no longer fun. Rebelling,*
*drinking, smoking, and more. I was scared*
*because it shrank the size of that door.*

*Oh Lord, please! Sanctify my soul!*

*Getting through that door is my ultimate goal. Lost some family, lost some friends. The saddest thing is not knowing where did they end.*

*Thanks to Jesus, I get to choose! No more smoking, no more booze. This is one battle I refuse to lose. I know which door that I will pick. Because His blood in me runs very thick!*

# Introduction

The title of this book may have startled you. Maybe you picked it up because the words *Suicide Letters* felt heavy, unsettling, or even dangerous. But this book isn't about dying in despair, it's about dying to the lies that keep us captive so that we can finally live free.

I never imagined I would write a book called *Suicide Letters.* For years, my life was marked by rejection, abuse, violation, betrayal, addiction, homelessness, and pain so deep that I often believed the only way out was to end my life. Those experiences became the breeding ground for lies. Lies about who I was, what I was worth, and whether I even had a future.

I once believed that ending my life would end my pain. But God showed me that the death I needed wasn't the end of my existence, it was the end of my bondage. I didn't need to die ashamed; I needed the shame in me to die. I didn't need to die in hopelessness; I needed to let hopelessness die in me. What the enemy meant for my destruction, God used as the soil for my deliverance. Through His mercy, I discovered that I didn't have to die in despair. Instead, I could die to my flesh, surrender my wounds, and find new life in

Christ. The life I was searching for was waiting on the other side of surrender.

That's what this book is about: surrender. Every chapter confronts one of the strongholds that once held me captive: rejection, abuse, shame, violation, fear, abandonment, addiction, betrayal, bitterness, poverty, hopelessness, and unforgiveness. I call them the *"dirty dozen"* strongholds that once buried my peace and buried my worth. You'll see how these battles played out in my own story, how they echo through the lives of people in Scripture, and how God calls each of us to surrender them through spiritual healing.

At the end of every chapter, you'll be invited to write your own "suicide letter."

These aren't letters of despair, they are letters of deliverance. They are love letters to God and to your own soul, declaring that the lies of the flesh must die so that the Spirit of God can live fully within you.

Here's what you can expect as you walk through these pages:

- You'll recognize the wounds that have shaped your life.
- You'll walk through the stages of surrender, much like the stages of grief, as you learn to die to your old self.

- You'll replace lies with God's promises by declaring His Word over your life.
- And finally, you'll experience freedom. Not just as an idea, but as a reality you can live in.

This book is my testimony, but it's also a roadmap for you. My prayer is that as you read, you'll see yourself in these pages. You'll cry when you need to cry, write when you need to release, and shout God's promises when you need to declare victory.

So, let's begin. Let's die to what has held us captive. Let's surrender every stronghold. Let's write these *suicide letters*, not as goodbyes to life; but as love letters to God and to ourselves, choosing once and for all to live in faith, freedom, and Spirit. ~*Maria Davila*

## Chapter 1: Rejection – Leah's Story

Rejection is a wound that cuts deeper than most people ever realize. For me, it began before I ever drew my first breath. My very existence was met with resistance, anger, and bitterness. My mother carried me in her womb with the weight of violation, trauma, and resentment pressing down on her heart. My father, instead of being a protector, had already tried to erase me before I was even born. Nine months pregnant, she carried me while he hoped for my end and physically tried to make that happen. That kind of rejection sinks into your bones, shaping the way you see the world long before you even understand what the world is.

As a child, I didn't need words to tell me I was unwanted. I could feel it in the air I breathed. It was in the glances, the silence, and the heavy cloud of bitterness that followed me everywhere I went. Rejection doesn't always shout; sometimes it whispers, and those whispers become the loudest voices inside your mind. *You're not enough. You don't belong. You were never meant to be here.* These lies became the lens through which I saw myself.

Rejection grows like a vine. It wraps around your heart, your choices, and your identity until it feels like part of who you are. I chased love in places where it was never safe. I longed for belonging so badly that I tolerated mistreatment just to feel chosen, even for a moment. I was like a child knocking on door after door, praying someone would open it and finally say, *"Come in. Stay. You matter."* But the doors seemed to stay closed, and the ache grew deeper.

When I read about Leah in Genesis 29, I felt like I was staring into a mirror. Leah wasn't the beautiful one, not the favored one. She was given to Jacob as a wife through deception, forced into a marriage where she was never truly loved. Every day she lived with the comparison of Rachel, her sister, adored and desired, while she remained in the shadows. Can you imagine the weight of lying next to your husband at night, knowing his heart belongs to someone else? Leah's rejection wasn't hidden; it was her daily reality.

And yet, in Leah's pain, God was moving. With each child she bore, it was as if she was crying out, *"Now my husband will love me! Now I will be seen!"* But it didn't happen. Jacob's heart never shifted. Still, God saw Leah. He saw her tears, her longing, her ache to belong. And in His sovereignty, it was Leah; the unwanted one who became the mother of Judah, the very line through which Jesus, the Savior of the world, would one day come. The rejected one was chosen by God for something eternal.

That truth changed me. I began to realize that rejection, as crushing as it felt, was never the end of my story. What others failed to see in me, God had already called forth. The places where I was pushed aside were the very places God planned to plant His purpose. He took the word *unwanted* that was stamped across my life and rewrote it with His hand: *chosen.*

But healing didn't come in an instant. It came through a process of surrender, of dying to the lies that rejection had built inside me. I had to look denial in the face and say, *"Yes, this hurt me. Yes, it shaped me. But it will not define me anymore."* I had to release the anger I held toward those who failed me, let go of the bargaining and the endless *"if only they had loved me differently"* and grieve the love I never received. Only then could I accept the truth: even if my mother and father forsake me, the Lord Himself will receive me.

Psalm 27:10 became more than words on a page; it became my anchor. When the memories tried to drag me back into despair, I would whisper it like a lifeline: *"Though my father and mother forsake me, the Lord will receive me."* Each time I said it, rejection lost a little more power over me.

## Deliverance Exercise: Breaking Free from Rejection

### *Step 1: Recognize the Root*

Think back to the first time you remember feeling unwanted. Was it a parent's words, a teacher's dismissal, a friend turning their back on you? Write down that memory. Be honest. Recognition begins with naming the wound.

### *Step 2: Feel the Ache*

Leah longed for Jacob's love, just as you may have longed for the love of someone who withheld it. Allow yourself to feel that ache for a moment. Say aloud: *"I wanted their love, but I didn't receive it."* This simple confession breaks denial and opens the door to healing.

### *Step 3: Release the Anger*

Rejection often breeds anger at others, at yourself, even at God. Speak it out: *"I was angry when they overlooked me. I was angry when they chose someone else over me. I was angry when I felt invisible."* Releasing it doesn't excuse what happened, but it keeps anger from becoming bitterness.

### *Step 4: Surrender the 'What Ifs'*

Leah said, *"Now my husband will love me,"* but her hope was never met. How many times have you whispered, *"If only they had chosen me, if only they had loved me differently...* "? Write down one of your "if onlys." Then, cross it out and declare: *"I cannot change the past, but I surrender it to God today."*

### *Step 5: Step into Freedom*

Read Psalm 27:10 aloud: *"Though my father and mother forsake me, the Lord will receive me."* You can replace mother and father with the name or title of someone else. Example *"Though my husband/wife forsake me, the Lord will receive me."* Speak it three times. Let your ears hear the truth your heart has longed to believe. You are not forsaken. You are received. You are chosen.

## *Write Yourself a Letter of Surrender: Example Rejection*

Dear Father,

Today I choose to surrender rejection from (Name)_____. From the womb until now, I've carried the lies that I am unwanted. But I no longer want to live under its power. I put to death the lie that I am unworthy of love. I bury it at the cross where Jesus bore my shame. Instead, I receive Your promise: *"Though my father and mother forsake me, the Lord will receive me"* (Psalm 27:10). I belong to You. This is my breakup letter to the flesh that I will no longer live in, and my love letter to You. I choose to live by faith, walk in freedom, and embrace the new life You have given me.

In Jesus' name, Amen.

## Chapter 2: Abuse & Violence – Moses' Story

Abuse has a way of leaving invisible scars that throb long after the bruises fade. Violence is more than the breaking of bones; it is the shattering of trust, the crushing of innocence, and the stealing of safety. My story of abuse began before I had language for it, before I could defend myself or even cry out. My father, the one who should have been my shield, became the one who tried to end my life before it even began. Nine months in my mother's womb, I was already a target of violence. That attempt at erasing me, though it failed, left its mark on my soul. I entered this world already acquainted with the feeling of being unsafe.

Growing up, that sense of danger never strayed far. I learned quickly that love was unpredictable and often dangerous. The hands that should have held me gently could also strike. Words were weapons, sharper than knives. Even silence could be violent, stretching out like a storm cloud ready to break. Abuse conditions you to anticipate harm even in moments of calm. You learn to flinch at kindness, to question motives, to brace yourself for the next blow.

And yet, in the middle of that darkness, I see reflections of another story: the story of

Moses in Exodus 1-2. Born into a world where his very life was threatened by Pharaoh's decree, Moses entered existence marked for death. Every Hebrew boy was to be thrown into the Nile, his cries drowned out by the waters of a nation's fear. Imagine his mother's desperation as she hid him for three months, her heart pounding with every sound, every knock, every whisper in the streets. She built a basket, smeared it with tar, and released her baby into the river, an act of both terror and faith. Violence surrounded him, but God's hand carried him.

Moses grew up in Pharaoh's palace, surrounded by the very empire that tried to destroy him. He witnessed oppression firsthand, watching his people beaten and broken by the whip. The rage of injustice flared in him one day as he saw an Egyptian strike a Hebrew slave, and Moses reacted. That's when his own hands became instruments of violence as he killed the Egyptian and buried him in the sand. Abuse had surrounded his story so long, it bled into his own choices. Yet even in his failures, God was not finished with him.

This is the paradox of abuse and violence: it seeks to end you, but God can transform even your most broken beginnings into a story of deliverance. Just as God raised Moses to lead His people out of bondage, He has the power to take our scars and turn them into testimonies. What began with violence can end in victory.

But healing from abuse requires courage. It means naming what happened without flinching, even when your voice trembles. It means stepping out of denial, confronting anger, and surrendering the urge to repeat the cycle. It means acknowledging the losses abuse has stolen from you: your safety, your innocence, your trust and allowing God to restore what was taken.

## Deliverance Exercise: Breaking Free from Abuse & Violence

### *Step 1: Recognize the Violation*

Think back to a time when you felt unsafe, threatened, or harmed. It may have been physical, emotional, or even the violence of words. Write it down. Naming the violation is the first step toward breaking its power.

### *Step 2: Acknowledge the Fear*

Like Moses' mother hiding him, you may have lived in constant fear. Speak it out: *"I was afraid when..."* and finish the sentence. Let the fear come into the light where God can meet you.

### Step 3: Release the Anger

Abuse stirs anger at the abuser, at yourself, at the unfairness of it all. Say aloud: *"I was angry because they hurt me. I was angry because I deserved safety and didn't have it."* Releasing anger is not excusing the abuse; it is refusing to let it poison your future.

### Step 4: Grieve the Loss

Abuse robs us of more than moments; it steals trust, innocence, and peace. Take a quiet moment to grieve what you lost. Whisper a prayer: *"Lord, I mourn the safety I never knew, the love that was twisted, the trust that was broken."*

### *Step 5: Step into Protection*

Read Psalm 91:4 aloud: *"He will cover you with His feathers, and under His wings you will find refuge."* Repeat it three times. Close your eyes. Imagine yourself safe beneath His wings, covered, defended, and cherished.

## *Write Yourself a Letter of Surrender: Example Abuse & Violence*

Dear Father,

Today I choose to surrender the abuse and violence that marked my life. I confess the fear, the anger, and the pain I have carried for far too long. I no longer want to live under its shadow. I put to death the lie that I will never be safe. I bury it at the cross where Jesus took every blow meant for me. Instead, I receive Your promise: *"He will cover you with His feathers, and under His wings you will find refuge"* (Psalm 91:4). You are my protector, my refuge, my defender. This is my letter to the flesh that

seeks to keep me captive, I'm letting it go.
This is my love letter to You. I choose to
live by faith, to walk in safety, and to
embrace the freedom You have secured for
me.

In Jesus' name, Amen.

## Chapter 3: Shame – The Woman at the Well

Shame is a shadow that clings to your soul, whispering that you are unworthy, unwanted, and unforgivable. Unlike rejection, which comes from others pushing you away, shame digs its claws into your own heart and convinces you to hide. I know this shadow well. For years, I carried the weight of things that were done to me and choices I made in response to my pain. I buried them deep, afraid that if anyone saw the truth, they would confirm what shame had already told me: *"You are ruined. You are unlovable. You are too far gone."*

It didn't take much for shame to weave itself into my identity. A cutting remark from someone who should have cared. A secret violation left unspoken. The choices I made when I was desperate for relief but ended up only adding more pain. Shame doesn't just remember what you did; it brands you by it. It doesn't say you messed up. It says, You ARE the mess. And so, I learned to smile while hiding the parts of me that ached the most. I became skilled at pretending, while inside I felt like a hollow shell.

One day, I read about the woman at the well in John 4, and it was as though the pages themselves breathed life into my lungs. This woman knew shame. She came to the well at noon, the hottest part of the day, when no one else would be there. Why? Because she was tired of the whispers, the side-eyes, the gossip that followed her wherever she went. Married five times, now living with a man who wasn't her husband she wore her shame like a scarlet letter. So, she chose isolation, carrying her water jar alone, hoping to avoid the condemnation of others.

But Jesus was waiting for her. Not by accident, but by divine appointment. He sat by that well knowing her story, knowing the shame that weighed on her shoulders, and still, He engaged her in conversation.

Imagine her surprise when a Jewish man spoke to her a Samaritan woman. Imagine her discomfort as He exposed her truth, not to shame her further but to show her that He saw her completely and still offered her living water. He told her everything she had ever done, and instead of condemning her, He invited her into freedom. The very woman who came to the well hiding from her community ran back into town to tell everyone about Jesus. The one who hid in shame became the messenger of hope.

That's the power of God's love. Shame tells us to hide, but Jesus meets us in the hiding places and calls us into the light. He doesn't deny our failures; He redeems them. He doesn't cover up our scars; He transforms them into testimonies. Like the woman at the well, I learned that what I tried to bury in secrecy, God wanted to bring into the open so He could heal it. And in that healing, the lies of shame began to lose their grip on me.

## Deliverance Exercise: Breaking Free from Shame

### *Step 1: Identify the Secret*

Think of one thing you've hidden from others out of fear of judgment. Write it down in a private place. Naming the secret removes some of shame's power.

### *Step 2: Confront the Lie*

Shame says, "*I am ruined. I am too far gone.*" Say out loud: "*I am not my mistakes. I am not what was done to me.*" Let truth confront the lie.

### Step 3: Picture the Well

Close your eyes and imagine yourself at the well with Jesus. He looks at you, knowing your whole story. Hear Him say, "*I see you, and I offer you living water.*" Stay in that moment until you feel His acceptance settle into your heart.

### Step 4: Grieve the Mask

Think about the ways you've hidden your true self because of shame. Whisper a prayer: "*Lord, I grieve the years I spent hiding. Help me step into the light of Your love.*"

### Step 5: Step into Radiance

Read Psalm 34:5 aloud: "*Those who look to Him are radiant; their faces are never covered with shame.*" Repeat it three times. Believe that this promise is yours.

### *Write Yourself a Letter of Surrender: Example Shame*

Dear Father,

Today I surrender the shame that has followed me like a shadow. I confess the secrets I've hidden, the masks I've worn, and the lies I've believed in myself. I no longer want to live under its weight. I put to death the lie that I am ruined beyond repair. I bury it at the cross where Jesus bore my guilt and shame. Instead, I receive Your promise: *"Those who look to Him are radiant; their faces are never covered with shame"* (Psalm 34:5). You call me Radiant, and I choose to walk in that light.  This is my letter to the flesh that clings to secrecy, my love letter to You. I choose to bring it to the surface and live in honesty, freedom, and the radiance of Your grace.

In Jesus' name, Amen.

## Chapter 4: Violation – Tamar's Story

There are wounds so deep, words struggle to contain them. Rape is one of those wounds. It does not just touch the body; it invades the soul, steals innocence, and leaves behind a silence that screams. For years, I carried this wound in secret. My Uncle E forced himself on me, and I buried the memory so far down that I almost convinced myself it wasn't real. But the body remembers. The soul remembers. Silence does not erase the pain; it only chains it tighter.

As a teenage girl, I did not have the language for what was happening. I only knew the confusion, the fear, the way my heart pounded when I heard his name. I remember staring at the walls, wishing I could disappear, trying to kick and push him away.

When it was over, I was left with an unbearable shame, the kind that convinces you it was somehow your fault. I tried to tell my aunt, she told me it was my fault, I shouldn't have been there with the family drinking. She also warned me if I told anyone it would cause war in our family, and anyone getting hurt would be my fault. I believed in every lie; and I kept it quiet.

That shame followed me into womanhood, whispering lies about my worth, my innocence, my value. It told me I was ruined, that no one could ever love me if they knew the truth.

When I read Tamar's story in 2 Samuel 13, I felt an ache so familiar it was as if the pages of Scripture reached out and touched my own hidden scars. Tamar was a young woman, innocent, and full of promise. Her half-brother Amnon burned with lust for her, and through deception he lured her into his chamber. She pleaded with him, begged him not to violate her, but he overpowered her and raped her.

Afterward, he cast her aside with hatred greater than the lust that had driven him.

Tamar tore her robe and wept loudly, her dignity ripped from her along with her innocence. And then, silence. Her brother Absalom told her to keep quiet, to not let it be known. The Bible says, *"Tamar lived in her brother Absalom's house, desolate."*

That word, desolate; is what rape leaves behind. A hollow emptiness. A silence heavy with shame. Tamar's story is not tied with a neat bow. There is no sudden resolution, no immediate justice. She lives in the ruins of what was done to her. And for so many of us who have endured sexual violation, we know that feeling well.

But here is what I have learned: silence is the soil where shame grows, but truth is the place where healing begins. For years I was desolate, too. But God met me in my silence. He taught me that what happened to me was not my fault. He showed me that my body, though violated, was still His temple, still precious in His sight. And He began to speak a better word over me: beloved, chosen, redeemed. Like Tamar, my story did not resolve quickly, but unlike Tamar, I refused to remain desolate. By bringing my story into the light, by telling the truth of what happened, I found the first steps of freedom.

Rape is not the end of your story. It is not the definition of who you are. What was stolen can be restored, and what was broken can be healed. God is a defender of the violated, and He binds up the wounds of the brokenhearted.

## Deliverance Exercise: Breaking Free from Violation

### Step 1: Name the Violation

If you have carried sexual trauma in silence, take a deep breath and whisper the truth to God. Say: "*Lord, this happened to me, and I need Your healing.*" Naming it out loud is the beginning of breaking its chains.

### Step 2: Confront the Lies

Rape tells you it was your fault, that you are ruined, that you are unclean. Say aloud: "*It was not my fault. I am not ruined. I am not unclean.*" Write these words down and circle them as your declaration of truth.

### Step 3: Release the Shame

Shame thrives in secrecy. Imagine yourself handing the weight of shame to Jesus. Whisper: *"Lord, I give You the shame I have carried. I refuse to hide anymore."*

### Step 4: Grieve the Loss

It is okay to weep for everything that was stolen: innocence, trust, dignity. Cry if you need to. Pray: *"Lord, I grieve what was taken, but I believe You can restore my soul."*

### Step 5: Step into Healing

Read Psalm 147:3 aloud: *"He heals the brokenhearted and binds up their wounds."* Repeat it three times. Picture God gently binding the wounds of your heart, wrapping you in His love and healing.

## Write Yourself a Letter of Surrender: Example Sexual Violation

Dear Father,

Today I surrendered the violation that has haunted me. I confess the silence, the shame, and the lies I believed about myself. I no longer want to live desolate, hidden, or broken. I put to death the lie that I am ruined beyond repair. I bury it at the cross where Jesus bore my pain. Instead, I receive Your promise: *"He heals the brokenhearted and binds up their wounds"* (Psalm 147:3). You are my Healer, my Restorer, my Redeemer. This is my letter to the flesh that carries shame, my love letter to You. I choose to walk in dignity, freedom, and healing.

In Jesus' name, Amen.

## Chapter 5: Fear – Gideon's Story

Fear is a prison without visible walls. It doesn't chain your wrists or your ankles, but it binds your mind and suffocates your heart. I have known fear in its many disguises: the fear of being hurt again, the fear of being abandoned, the fear of failing, and even the fear of succeeding. Fear whispers, "*Stay small, stay hidden, stay quiet.*" It convinces you that safety lies in invisibility, that silence is protection. But fear is a lie.

My earliest memories are marked by fear. Fear of my father's violence. Fear of rejection from my mother. Fear of being unwanted, unsafe, unseen. Fear became the air I breathed. Even when I grew older, it followed me. I feared making the wrong choice. I feared stepping out of line. And perhaps most of all, I feared the future. Would I ever break free from the cycle of pain? Or was I doomed to repeat the same story over and over again?

When I read the story of Gideon in Judges 6, I saw myself in him. The Bible says Gideon was threshing wheat in a winepress. That image is strange. A man doing the work of threshing wheat. This should have been done in an open field. Instead, he was hiding in a pit carved out to press grapes. Why? Because he was afraid.

The Midianites were oppressing Israel, and Gideon was terrified of being discovered, terrified of losing what little he had. So, he worked in secret, hiding in fear.

But it was in that very place of fear that the angel of the Lord appeared to him and spoke words that must have sounded impossible: "*The Lord is with you, mighty warrior.*" Mighty warrior? Gideon, who was hiding in a hole, trembling at the thought of his enemies? God wasn't speaking to Gideon's fear; He was speaking to Gideon's destiny. He saw beyond the shaking hands and the fearful heart. He saw a leader, a deliverer, a man who would rise up in God's strength.

I can only imagine Gideon's confusion. He even argued back, pointing out his weakness, his insignificance, his doubts. But God's answer was steady: "*I will be with you.*" Gideon's courage was not rooted in his own ability but in God's presence. And that truth began to change him. The man who once hid in fear became the man who led Israel into victory, not because he was fearless, but because he chose faith over fear.

I stood in my own winepresses, hiding from what scared me. Opportunities I felt unworthy of, relationships I didn't trust, callings I felt too weak to fulfill. Fear told me to stay small. But God's voice, steady and firm, whispered, "*I am with you. You are stronger than you know. You are chosen for more.*" Slowly, I began to rise out of the pit.

### Deliverance Exercise: Breaking Free from Fear

#### *Step 1: Identify the Fear*

What is the fear that has controlled you the most? Write it down plainly: "I am afraid of..." Naming it diminishes its hidden power.

#### *Step 2: Picture the Winepress*

Imagine yourself like Gideon, hiding in a pit, clinging to scraps. Ask yourself: *"What am I hiding from right now? Where has fear kept me small?"* Write your answer honestly.

### Step 3: Hear God's Words

Whisper aloud: "*The Lord is with me; he calls me a mighty warrior.*" Say it slowly. Repeat it until the words begin to sink in. God is calling out your destiny, not your fear.

### Step 4: Release the Control

Fear often tries to control outcomes. Take a moment to open your hands as a symbol. Pray: "*Lord, I release control. I cannot predict or protect everything, but I choose to trust You.*"

### Step 5: Step into Courage

Read Psalm 23:4 aloud: "*Even though I walk through the darkest valley, I will fear no evil, for You are with me."* Repeat it three times. Each time, say it louder, stronger, as a declaration that you will not live in fear.

### *Write Yourself a Letter of Surrender: Example Fear*

Dear Father,

Today I surrender fear. I confess the ways it has controlled my choices, silenced my voice, and kept me small. I no longer want to live in the shadows of fear. I put to death the lie that I am powerless and unprotected. I bury it at the cross where Jesus conquered every enemy. Instead, I receive Your promise: "*Even though I walk through the darkest valley, I will fear no evil, for You are with me*" (Psalm 23:4). You are my courage and my strength. This is my letter to the flesh that trembles in fear, my love letter to You. I choose to rise as the warrior You see in me, to walk in faith, and to trust Your presence every step of the way.

In Jesus' name, Amen.

## Chapter 6: Abandonment – Joseph's Story

Abandonment is a wound that whispers, *"You are not worth staying for."* It cuts deep when those who should have loved us, protected us, and stood by us instead turned away, walked out, or left us behind. My life has known that wound too well. From the earliest days, I felt the sting of being left emotionally by my parents, even while physically present. And as I grew, abandonment echoed through friendships, relationships, and even places I thought were safe. Each leaving confirmed the lie: *"You are disposable. You are easy to walk away from."*

Abandonment doesn't just hurt once; it lingers. It makes you flinch at love, waiting for it to leave. It makes you hold people at a distance, telling yourself it's better not to need anyone. It makes you sabotage what's good because you assume it will end anyway. The wound is not just about the people who left; it's about how deeply you believe you are unworthy of someone staying.

When I read Joseph's story in Genesis 37, it is impossible not to see abandonment at the center of his pain. He was the favored son of Jacob, gifted with a coat of many colors, marked for destiny. But his own brothers, consumed by jealousy, plotted against him. They threw him into a pit, cold and empty, listening to his cries for help. Can you hear his voice echoing off the walls of that pit? *"Don't leave me here! Please!"* Yet they sat down to eat while he begged for his life. Then, with hard hearts, they sold him into slavery, watching him be carried away in chains. Joseph's abandonment wasn't subtle, it was betrayal by blood, rejection by family, the deepest wound a soul can know.

And yet, the story doesn't end in the pit. Joseph was abandoned by his brothers, forgotten in prison, but never forsaken by God. Every time the world turned its back, the Scriptures remind us: *"But the Lord was with Joseph."* Even when people walked away, God's presence never left him. In time, Joseph rose from the prison to the palace, from forgotten to favored, from abandoned to entrusted with the destiny of nations. The very brothers who left him to die one day bowed before him, and Joseph could say, *"You meant it for evil, but God meant it for good."*

I see myself in Joseph's pit crying out for someone to stay, only to hear footsteps walking away. But like Joseph, I am learning that God's presence is the constant no one can steal. Though others leave, He remains. Though others turn away, His eyes stay fixed on me. Though others forget, He remembers.

## Deliverance Exercise: Breaking Free from Abandonment

### Step 1: Recall the Leaving

Think back to a moment when someone important left you: a parent, a spouse, a friend. Write down what you felt at that moment. Naming it is the first step toward healing.

### Step 2: Feel the Pit

Close your eyes and imagine Joseph in the pit, calling out for help. Picture yourself in your own "pit of abandonment." Say aloud: *"This is how it felt when they left me."* Allow yourself to grieve it.

### *Step 3: Release the Lie*

Abandonment tells you, "*You are unworthy. You are disposable.*" Speak against it: "*I am not disposable. I am precious to God, and He never leaves me.*"

### *Step 4: Invite God's Presence*

Pray: "*Lord, sit with me in my pit. Remind me that You are here, even when others left.*" Breathe in His presence and let His nearness replace the loneliness.

### *Step 5: Step into Assurance*

Read Psalm 139:9–10 aloud: "*If I rise on the wings of the dawn, if I settle on the far side of the sea, even there Your hand will guide me, Your right hand will hold me fast*." Repeat it three times. Let it wash over you like a promise you can cling to.

## Write Yourself a Letter of Surrender: Example Abandonment

Dear Father,

Today I surrender the pain of abandonment. I confess the wounds of those who left me, the loneliness that filled the silence, and the lies I believed because of it. I no longer want to live chained to the fear of being left. I put to death the lie that I am disposable and unworthy of love. I bury it at the cross where Jesus was forsaken so I would never be.

Instead, I receive Your promise: *"Even there Your hand will guide me, Your right hand will hold me fast" (Psalm 139:9–10)*. You have never left me, and You never will. This is my letter to the flesh that trembles at abandonment, my love letter to You. I choose to rest in Your presence, to trust Your hand, and to believe I am never alone.

In Jesus' name, Amen.

## Chapter 7: Bitterness – Naomi's Story

Bitterness begins as a seed. It's small, almost invisible; but if left untended, it grows into a thorny vine that wraps around the heart and squeezes out joy. It thrives in loss, betrayal, and disappointment, and once rooted, it poisons every thought and every relationship. I know the taste of bitterness well. Life's blows left me wounded, and in my anger, I let those wounds fester. Bitterness whispered to me that it was safer to be hard than to be hurt again. There were days when I could feel bitterness rising in me like bile. Every memory of rejection, every betrayal, every violation seemed to replay in my mind like an endless film reel. Instead of healing, I rehearsed my pain. I wore my anger like armor, convincing myself it protected me, but really it only kept love out. Bitterness made me cynical, mistrustful, and closed off. And though it felt like strength, it was a prison of my own making.

When I read Naomi's story in the book of Ruth, I recognized that same bitterness. Naomi lost her husband, then both of her sons. In her grief, she told the women of Bethlehem, *"Don't call me Naomi. Call me Mara, because the Almighty has made my life very bitter."* Naomi's name meant "*pleasant*," but she no longer believed that described her life. Bitterness had redefined her identity. She returned home feeling empty, convinced God Himself had turned against her.

And yet, even in her bitterness, God was not finished with Naomi. She could not see it at the time, but Ruth, her Moabite daughter-in-law who clung to her, would become the channel of her restoration. Ruth's loyalty, courage, and faithfulness positioned Naomi to become part of a story greater than her pain. Through Ruth's marriage to Boaz came Obed, the grandfather of King David, the lineage of Christ Himself. Out of Naomi's bitterness,

God brought a blessing beyond what she could have ever imagined.

Naomi's story reminds me that bitterness is not final. It may rename us, it may weigh us down, but it cannot cancel God's redemptive plan. He knows how to turn mourning into dancing, how to restore joy where sorrow has lived for years. The bitterness that once felt like my identity is being replaced with the sweetness of His grace.

## Deliverance Exercise: Breaking Free from Bitterness

### Step 1: Identify the Root

Think of a moment when bitterness took hold, perhaps after betrayal, loss, or repeated disappointments. Write down the memory that planted the seed.

### Step 2: Feel the Weight

Whisper Naomi's words: "*The Almighty has made my life very bitter.*" Allow yourself to feel the heaviness of carrying bitterness for so long. Acknowledge that it has shaped your outlook.

### Step 3: Release the Accusation

Bitterness often accuses God or others of being the cause of our pain. Say aloud: "*I release my accusation. Lord, I don't understand everything, but I choose to trust You.*"

### Step 4: Grieve What Was Lost

Like Naomi, you may have lost people, opportunities, or years. Take time to grieve them. Pray: "*Lord, I mourn the years I spent in anger, but I trust You can restore joy.*"

### Step 5: Step into Joy

Read Psalm 30:11 aloud: "*You turned my mourning into dancing; You removed my sackcloth and clothed me with joy.*" Repeat it three times. Imagine the heaviness lifting and joy clothing you instead.

### *Write Yourself a Letter of Surrender:*
### *Example Bitterness*

Dear Father,

Today I surrender bitterness. I confess the anger I have carried, the grudges I have nursed, and the hardness of heart that grew in me. I no longer want to live defined by my wounds. I put to death the lie that my life will always be bitter. I bury it at the cross where Jesus carried all my sorrows. Instead, I receive Your promise: "*You turned my mourning into dancing; You removed my sackcloth and clothed me with joy*" (Psalm 30:11). You are restoring joy to my soul. This is my letter to the flesh that clings to bitterness, my love letter to You. I choose to walk in forgiveness, freedom, and the sweetness of Your grace.

In Jesus' name, Amen.

## Chapter 8: Betrayal – Jesus' Story

Betrayal is one of the deepest cuts the human heart can endure. It is not the strike of an enemy that wounds the most, but the sting of a friend's kiss. The closer the bond, the sharper the pain. I know betrayal, the moments when people I trusted, some I loved, turned against me. The shock of it left me gasping, as if the ground had crumbled beneath my feet. It made me question everything: my judgment, my worth, even my faith in people. It started off softly. Not with a knife, but with a smile. Not with an attack, but with an invitation.

For me, it began at the chamber; a place meant for community, connection, and support. A place where people shake hands, exchange cards, and talk about collaboration. I walked in believing God would send the right people. What I didn't see was that the enemy was sending people too. People drawn not by the mission God gave us, but by the platform they could take from it. I thought they were allies. I thought they saw my heart. I thought they cared about the mission of the ministry. Instead, they were watching our growth. Looking for a way in. And just when the organization was climbing, just when we were stretching to meet the needs of the people God called us to serve, everything changed.

Simultaneously, three individuals with their own dark agendas began to infiltrate our organization. We had our own modern-day Jezebel, Judas, and a Serpent. I write about it in my book Homeless Hero because it marked a turning point in my life and my ministry. It wasn't an enemy who wounded me. It was someone who once looked me in the eye at a chamber event, smiled, and said, "Let's be friends." That betrayal brought on a unique kind of loneliness. You don't just lose people; you lose the trust that was the very foundation of relationships.

I remember the nights I stared at the ceiling, unable to sleep, replaying the words and actions of those who had set out to hurt me. The betrayal wasn't just what they did. It was in the thought that they stepped into my life. They said they wanted to help and they admired the mission God gave me. I opened the door. I welcomed them in and I trusted them with the heart of the ministry. They ate at my table. They witnessed miracles. They heard my prayers. They saw my exhaustion. They knew the weight I carried. They could look at me in the eye, smile, and still walk away with a dagger hidden behind their back.

When I look to Scripture, I see betrayal written across the story of Jesus. Judas, one of His own disciples, walked with Him for years. He witnessed the miracles, heard the teachings, shared meals with the Son of God. And yet, for thirty pieces of silver, Judas betrayed Him with a kiss. That kiss in Gethsemane still echoes through history as the ultimate act of deception; a moment of intimacy turned into weapon.

But Judas was not the only one. Peter, the bold disciple who swore he would never leave, denied Him three times when the pressure mounted. The other disciples scattered, abandoning Him in His darkest hour. Jesus stood trial mocked and beaten, bearing the weight of betrayal not only by His friends but by the very people He came to save. And yet, from the cross, He spoke words that shatter the power of betrayal:

"Father, forgive them, for they know not what they do."

That is the difference between human response and divine grace. Betrayal tempts us toward bitterness, vengeance, and self-protection. But Jesus showed us another way. The way of surrender, the way of forgiveness, and the way of trusting in our Father's plan even when people fail. His story reminds us that betrayal cannot destroy destiny. What others mean for evil, God can turn for good.

I've learned this in my own life and betrayal was not the end of my story. It was the refining fire that removed people who were drilling holes in the ark, and it drove me closer to God. He will never betray me.

People may walk away, but God remains.
Friends may fail, but Jesus is faithful.
Betrayal temporarily broke me, but it has
also built in me a deeper reliance on Him
who restored me.

## Deliverance Exercise: Breaking Free from Betrayal

### *Step 1: Remember the Betrayal*

Think of the person who betrayed you: a friend, a spouse, a family member. Write down their name and what they did. Acknowledge it honestly. Betrayal must be named to be healed.

### *Step 2: Feel the Wound*

Allow yourself to feel the sting. Say aloud: "It hurt when they…" and complete the sentence. Admitting the wound breaks denial.

### *Step 3: Release the Anger*

Anger is natural after betrayal. Whisper: "Lord, I release the anger I carry against them. I will not let this poison me any longer."

### *Step 4: Choose Forgiveness*

Forgiveness is not excusing the betrayal; it is cutting the chain that ties you to the pain. Say: "Father, I choose to forgive them, just as You forgave me."

### *Step 5: Step into Faithfulness*

Read Psalm 41:9–10 aloud: "Even my close friend, someone I trusted, one who shared my bread, has turned against me. But

You, Lord, have mercy on me and raise me up." Repeat it three times. Let God's faithfulness cover the wound of betrayal.

## Write Yourself a Letter of Surrender: Example Betrayal

Dear Father, today I surrender the wound of betrayal. I confess the pain of those who turned against me, the anger that burned in my heart, and the mistrust that followed. I no longer want to live chained to the memory of their betrayal. I put to death the lie that I can never trust again. I bury it at the cross where Jesus forgave His betrayers. Instead, I receive Your promise: *"But You, Lord, have mercy on me and raise me up"* (Psalm 41:9–10). You are faithful even when people are not. This is my letter to the flesh that clings to vengeance, my love letter to You. I choose to forgive, to release, and to walk in the freedom of Your mercy.

In Jesus' name, Amen.

## Chapter 9: Addiction – The Prodigal Son

Addiction is a slow thief. It rarely storms in all at once; instead, it creeps in quietly, promising relief, escape, or just one moment of pleasure to dull the ache inside. But soon, what once felt like control became a chain. I know that chain. I know what it's like to numb the pain with whatever would silence the memories, even if only for a little while. Addiction whispers that you are in control, but the truth is, it always takes more than it gives. It steals dignity, drains hope, and leaves you emptier than before.

In my darkest seasons, addiction was not always a substance sometimes it was people, sometimes habits, sometimes toxic patterns that felt impossible to break. Anything to distract me from the rejection, the abuse, the shame. But addiction never truly satisfies. Hunger only grows, and guilt deepens with every compromise. I carried the weight of promises I made to myself "I'll never do this again" only to break them in moments of weakness. The shame of relapse became another chain wrapped tightly around me.

When I read the parable of the Prodigal Son in Luke 15, I saw myself in his reckless search for fulfillment. He demanded his inheritance, a bold declaration of independence, and then squandered it on wild living. For a while, it probably felt exhilarating — freedom, indulgence, escape. But when the money ran out, so did the friends. He found himself in a pigpen, filthy and starving, longing for scraps that even the pigs refused. That is where addiction always leads: a place of hunger, filth, and desperation.

But the turning point in his story is also where hope begins for us. The Bible says, "When he came to his senses…" It wasn't when he had money, or when he had friends, but when he had nothing left — that's when clarity broke through. He remembered his father's house, a place where even servants had more than enough. With humility, he resolved to return, not as a son but as a servant. What he didn't know was that the father was already watching, waiting, and ready to run to him.

That image has never left me. The father running down the road, arms open wide, not to scold or condemn, but to embrace. The robe, the ring, the feast — all symbols that the prodigal was not just welcomed back but restored. Addiction tells us we are too far gone, too broken to return. But God shows us that the moment we turn toward Him, He runs to us with love.

I know the pigpen. I know the despair of being enslaved to destructive patterns. But I also know the freedom of hearing the Father say, "You were lost, but now you are found. You were dead, but now you are alive."

Addiction does not have the final word.

God's love does.

## Deliverance Exercise: Breaking Free from Addiction

### *Step 1: Name the Chain*

What is the addiction that has bound you? It may be a substance, a habit, or a destructive relationship. Write it down honestly.

### *Step 2: Picture the Pigpen*

Imagine yourself in the place where your addiction has taken you — the lowest moment, the place of shame. Say aloud: "This is where my choices have led me." Acknowledging the pigpen is the first step toward leaving it.

### Step 3: Confront the Lie

Addiction tells you, "This is who you are. You can never be free." Speak against it: "I am not my addiction. I am a child of God, created for freedom."

### Step 4: Make the Turn

Pray: "Father, I come to my senses. I turn back to You, even if all I can offer is my brokenness." Imagine yourself walking toward Him, step by step.

### Step 5: Receive the Embrace

Read Psalm 18:16–17 aloud: "He reached down from on high and took hold of me; He drew me out of deep waters. He rescued me from my powerful enemy."

Repeat it three times. Picture God pulling you out of the pit and wrapping you in His embrace.

## Write Yourself a Letter of Surrender: Example Addiction

Dear Father, today I surrender the chains of addiction. I confess the habits, the patterns, and the cravings that have controlled me. I no longer want to live in the pigpen of shame. I put to death the lie that I am my addiction, that I will never be free. I bury it at the cross where Jesus broke every chain. Instead, I receive Your promise: "He reached down from on high and took hold of me; He drew me out of deep waters. He rescued me from my powerful enemy" (Psalm 18:16–17). You are my Rescuer and my Deliverer. This is my letter to the flesh that longs for chains, my love letter to You.

I choose freedom, restoration, and the joy of being found in Your arms.

In Jesus' name, Amen.

## Chapter 10: Poverty & Homelessness – David's Story

Poverty is not just the absence of money; it is the gnawing emptiness of insecurity. It is the fear of not knowing where the next meal will come from or if there will be a safe place to rest your head at night. Homelessness magnifies that fear, stripping you of dignity and leaving you exposed to the harshness of both the elements and people's judgments. I have walked through these shadows. I know what it feels like to carry every belonging in a bag, to search for shelter, to feel invisible in a world that passes by without seeing your need.

There were nights when the cold seeped into my bones, and loneliness was my only companion. Poverty made me feel less than human, as if my worth had been measured and found to be lacking. Homelessness whispers cruel lies: "You are forgotten. You are worthless. You are nothing." But even in those moments, when I felt stripped of everything, I discovered that God's presence could still find me. Poverty exposed my need, but it also positioned me to experience His provision.

David's story in 1 Samuel echoes this truth. Before he was a king, he was a fugitive. Saul's jealousy turned David from palace guests to hunted prey. With nowhere to go, David fled to caves dark, damp, and hidden. He knew the loneliness of homelessness, the fear of poverty, the sting of being an outcast. The anointed future king of Israel slept on stone floors and ate whatever scraps he could find. He wandered without safety, without stability, clinging to God's promises in the shadows.

And yet, in those caves, some of David's most powerful psalms were born. He cried out, "I am poor and needy, yet the Lord thinks upon me" (Psalm 40:17). His poverty did not disqualify him; it drew him into deeper dependence on God. His homelessness did not erase his calling; it prepared him for the crown. What looked like loss was shaping in him a heart after God's own heart.

I see myself in David's caves. I know the desperation of wondering how I would survive the next day. But I also know the miraculous ways God provided a meal when I was hungry, a stranger's kindness, a door that opened at just the right moment. Each act of provision reminded me that I was not forgotten. Poverty tried to define me as worthless, but God redefined me as His child.

## Deliverance Exercise: Breaking Free from Poverty & Homelessness

Step 1: Recall the Scarcity

Think back to a moment when you felt the sting of hunger, homelessness, or not having enough. Write it down honestly.

Step 2: Face the Lie

Poverty tells you, "You are forgotten. You are worthless." Say aloud: "I am not forgotten. I am valuable in God's eyes."

Step 3: Picture the Cave

Imagine David in the cave, alone and afraid. Now picture yourself there. Whisper: "Even here, God is with me."

Step 4: Release the Fear

Pray: "Lord, I release the fear of lack. I trust you to provide for me as You did for David." Open your hands as a symbol of surrender.

Step 5: Step into Provision

Read Psalm 37:25 aloud: "I was young and now I am old, yet I have never seen the righteous forsaken or their children begging bread." Repeat it three times. Let the promise of God's provision sink into your spirit.

**Write Yourself a Letter of Surrender:
Example Poverty & Homelessness**

Dear Father,

Today I surrender the pain of poverty
and homelessness. I confess the fear, the
shame, and the lies I believed when I had
nothing. I no longer want to live under the
weight of scarcity. I put to death the lie that
I am forgotten and worthless. I bury it at the
cross where Jesus became poor so that I
could be rich in Your love. Instead, I receive
Your promise: "*I have never seen the
righteous forsaken or their children begging
bread*" (Psalm 37:25). You are my Provider,
my Sustainer, my Shelter. This is my letter
to the flesh that trembles in lack, my love

letter to You. I choose to live in trust, to walk in faith, and to rest in the abundance of Your provision.

In Jesus' name, Amen.

## Chapter 11: Hopelessness – Job's Story

Hopelessness is more than sadness. It is the crushing weight that whispers, "There is no way out. Nothing will ever change. Why even try?" I have known that feeling nights when the darkness pressed in so thick it felt like morning would never come. Hopelessness is not just the absence of light; it is the suffocating belief that light itself has died.

There were moments in my life when I felt swallowed whole by despair. Homelessness, betrayal, rejection, abuse, each wound piled upon the other until it seemed unbearable. I remember crying out to God, asking, "Where are You? Do You see me? Do You care?" Hopelessness convinces you that even heaven is silent. And yet, even in those desperate cries, something in me longed to believe that the silence wasn't the end of the story.

When I think of hopelessness in the Bible, no one embodies it more than Job. Job lost everything in a single sweeping storm — his wealth, his servants, his children. One messenger after another came with devastating news until all was gone. Then came the boils on his skin, the mockery of his community, the cold comfort of his friends, and even the bitter words of his wife: "Curse God and die." Imagine the weight of his grief, his body in pain, his heart shattered, his future in ruins. Job sat in ashes, scraping his wounds with broken pottery. That is the picture of hopelessness — stripped, broken, empty.

And yet, Job did not let go of God completely. His words were raw, even accusatory at times: "Why did I not perish at birth? Why is life given to those in misery?" (Job 3:11, 20). But even in his despair, a thread of faith ran through his cries: "Though He slay me, yet will I trust Him" (Job 13:15). Job's hopelessness was real, but it was not final. In time, God revealed Himself, not with easy answers, but with His overwhelming presence. And in the end,

Job's story was one of restoration double for his trouble, beauty for his ashes.

Hopelessness tells us we are forgotten. Job's story reminds us that God sees, even in the ashes. He may not remove the pain immediately, but He promises that the story is not over. The dawn is coming, even when the night feels endless.

## Deliverance Exercise: Breaking Free from Hopelessness

### Step 1: Name the Darkness

Think of a time when hopelessness whispered to you, when you felt like giving up. Write down the words you heard in your mind. Be honest about the despair.

### Step 2: Sit in the Ashes

Picture Job sitting in ashes, scraping his wounds. Imagine yourself there. Say aloud: "This is how hopelessness has felt in my life." Acknowledging the ashes is the beginning of rising from them.

### Step 3: Confront the Lie

Hopelessness says, "It will always be this way." Declare instead: "My story is not over. God has a future for me."

### Step 4: Cry Out to God

Pray honestly: "Lord, I feel hopeless, but I choose to cry out to You like Job did. Meet me in my ashes." Don't hold back; let your soul speak.

### Step 5: Step into Hope

Read Psalm 42:11 aloud: "Why, my soul, are you downcast? Why so disturbed within me? Put your hope in God, for I will yet praise Him, my Savior and my God." Repeat it three times, emphasizing the words "I will yet praise Him." Let hope rise as a declaration of faith.

## Write Yourself a Letter of Surrender: Example Hopelessness

Dear Father, today I surrender the heaviness of hopelessness. I confess the despair, the lies, and the silence that made me believe my story was over. I no longer want to live buried in ashes. I put to death the lie that nothing will ever change. I bury it at the cross where Jesus conquered death itself. Instead, I receive Your promise: "Put your hope in God, for I will yet praise Him, my Savior and my God" (Psalm 42:11). You are the dawn that breaks my night. This is my letter to the flesh that surrenders to despair, my love letter to You. I choose hope, I choose life, and I choose to believe that You are not finished with me.

In Jesus' name, Amen.

## Chapter 12: Unforgiveness – Stephen's Story

Unforgiveness is a silent poison. It seeps into the cracks of your soul and hardens your heart one drop at a time. It tells you that holding on to the hurt keeps you strong, that refusing to forgive somehow punishes the one who wronged you. But the truth is, unforgiveness is a chain that binds you, not them. I have known this poison. I have replayed the betrayals, the rejections, the words and wounds that marked me, over and over until the bitterness became part of me.

And every time I thought I was protecting myself by holding on, I was really locking myself in a prison.

Forgiveness does not come easy. It feels unfair to release someone who hurt you deeply, especially when they never apologized or acknowledged the pain. I wrestled with this for years. How do you forgive a father who tried to erase your existence? How do you forgive an uncle who violated you? How do you forgive the people who abandoned, betrayed, or mocked you? These questions burned in me until I realized that unforgiveness was not punishing them, it was punishing me. It was stealing my peace, my joy, and my freedom.

In Acts 7, we find the story of Stephen, the first Christian martyr. He preached with boldness, declaring the truth of Jesus to those who opposed him. His words cut to their hearts, and in rage, they dragged him out of the city and began to stone him. Imagine the hail of rocks, the crowd's fury, the crushing pain with each blow. And yet, in his final moments, Stephen lifted his eyes to heaven and saw Jesus standing at the right hand of God. With his dying breath, he prayed: "Lord, do not hold this sin against them." Even as death closed in, Stephen forgave. His spirit was free, even while his body was broken.

That prayer shakes me to my core. Forgiveness is not natural — it is supernatural. It is choosing to release someone into God's hands, to trust Him with justice, and to refuse to let hatred rule your heart. Forgiveness is not forgetting, excusing, or minimizing the pain. It is choosing freedom over bondage, healing over bitterness, life over death.

I have learned that forgiveness is not a one-time act but a journey. Some wounds require me to forgive daily, sometimes moment by moment. But each time I whisper, "Lord, I choose to forgive," I feel the chains loosen. The weight lifts, and peace flows in. Forgiveness is not for them; it is for me. It is the key that unlocks the prison of my soul.

### Deliverance Exercise: Breaking Free from Unforgiveness

### Step 1: Name the Offense

Write down the name of the person who hurt you and what they did. Be specific. Bringing it into the light breaks its hidden power.

### Step 2: Feel the Weight

Say aloud: "It hurt when…" and finish the sentence. Acknowledge the pain honestly, just as Stephen acknowledged his suffering.

### Step 3: Release the Judgment

Pray: "Lord, I release the right to seek revenge. I place this person and this pain in Your hands."

### Step 4: Choose Forgiveness

Say aloud: *"I forgive ___ for ___."* Fill in the blanks. Speak it even if your emotions resist. Forgiveness is an act of obedience before it is a feeling.

### Step 5: Step into Freedom

Read Psalm 103:10–12 aloud: "He does not treat us as our sins deserve or repay us according to our iniquities… as far as the east is from the west, so far has He removed our transgressions from us." Repeat it three times. Let God's mercy toward you empower your mercy toward others.

**Write Yourself a Letter of Surrender**:
**Example Unforgiveness**

Dear Father, today I surrender unforgiveness. I confess the names, the wounds, and the grudges I have carried. I no longer want to live chained to the past. I put to death the lie that holding on will protect me. I bury it at the cross where Jesus forgave His killers and Stephen forgave his persecutors. Instead, I receive Your promise: "As far as the east is from the west, so far have You removed my transgressions from me" (Psalm 103:10–12). Because I am forgiven, I choose to forgive.

This is my letter to the flesh that clings to bitterness, my love letter to You. I choose to walk in freedom, peace, and grace.

In Jesus' name, Amen.

## Closing Section

**Master Declaration of Freedom.**

This is the anthem of a soul set free. As you have walked through rejection, abuse, shame, fear, abandonment, bitterness, betrayal, addiction, poverty, hopelessness, and unforgiveness, you have laid them one by one at the feet of Jesus. Now, it is time to rise and declare the truth over your life:

I am no longer a prisoner of the past. I am not defined by what was done to me or by the mistakes I have made. I am a child of God, redeemed by the blood of Jesus, filled with His Spirit, and walking in His freedom.

The lies have died, the chains are broken, and the grave clothes are left behind. I am chosen, loved, healed, forgiven, and free. From this day forward, I choose life in the Spirit over death in the flesh. I declare freedom in my mind, healing in my heart, and strength in my spirit. In Christ, I am whole. In Christ, I am new. In Christ, I am free.

Read this declaration aloud until it burns in your spirit. Let it echo louder than the lies ever did.

## Commitment Page

Take a moment now to make your personal commitment before God. Write your name, the date, and these words as a seal over your journey:

Today, I committed to live surrendered. I choose to die to the lies that once held me captive and to live in the freedom Christ has given me. I will no longer walk in the shadows of rejection, abuse, shame, fear, abandonment, bitterness, betrayal, addiction, poverty, hopelessness, or unforgiveness. Instead, I will walk in truth, hope, forgiveness, love, and victory. This is my covenant with God, my declaration of faith, and my step into lasting freedom.

(Signature)

_____

(Date)

_____

## Final Suicide Letter of Surrender Scriptures for Strength & Renewal

- Isaiah 41:10 – "So do not fear, for I am with you; do not be dismayed, for I am your God. I will strength when you and help you; I will uphold you with my righteous right hand."

- Psalm 34:18 – "The Lord is close to the brokenhearted and saves those who are crushed in spirit.

- Romans 8:1 – "Therefore, there is now no condemnation for those who are in Christ Jesus."

- 2 Corinthians 5:17 – "Therefore, if anyone is in Christ, the new creation has come: The old has gone, the new is here!"

- John 8:36 – "So if the Son sets you free, you will be free indeed."

Read these verses daily. Speak to them aloud as declarations of truth until they drown out the lies of the enemy.

## Prayers for Different Seasons

- When you feel afraid: "Lord, remind me that You are with me. Replace my fear with courage, my anxiety with peace."

- When shame returns: "Jesus, thank You that You bore my shame on the cross. Help me to walk in Your radiance."

- When betrayal stings: "Father, I forgive as You forgave me. Heal my heart and teach me to trust again."

- When hopelessness whispers: "Holy Spirit, breathe life into me. Remind me that my story is not over."

- When you feel weak: "God, be my strength when I have none. Carry me and help me to stand in Your power."

## Resources for Healing & Hope

As you close this book, remember: your journey of surrender and freedom is not meant to be walked alone. God has surrounded you with His Spirit, His Word, and His people to strengthen you day by day. Below are practical tools and resources to help you continue living in victory.

### Hotlines & Support (U.S. Based)

- Suicide & Crisis Lifeline: Dial 988 (24/7 confidential support)
- National Sexual Assault Hotline (RAINN): 1-800-656-4673

- National Domestic Violence Hotline: 1-800-799-7233
- SAMHSA Helpline (Substance Abuse & Mental Health): 1-800-662-4357

If you live outside the U.S., please search for local hotlines and support organizations in your country. You are not alone, help is available.

## Support Groups & Ministries

- Celebrate Recovery: Christ-centered program for those struggling with hurts, habits, and hang-ups (www.celebraterecovery.com)
- GriefShare: Support groups for those grieving loss (www.griefshare.org)

• Local Church Small Groups: Find community and accountability in a faith-based setting.

• Christian Counselors Directory: (www.christiancounselordirectory.com)

## Journaling Prompts for Ongoing Healing

1. What lies have I believed in myself, and what truth from Scripture replaces them?

2. In what areas of my life do I still need to surrender control to God?

3. Who do I need to forgive, and how can I take one step toward forgiveness today?

4. How have I seen God's provision and protection in my story this week?

5. What declarations of freedom can I write and pray over myself daily?

## Final Encouragement

You have begun a journey of surrender, healing, and freedom. There will still be battles but remember this: you are no longer fighting alone. The same God who carried you through these pages will carry you through every tomorrow. Surround yourself with Scripture, prayer, and people who speak life. Return often to the letters you wrote in this book, reminding yourself of the chains you left at the cross.

Never forget: You are chosen. You are loved. You are free.

## Acknowledgments

First and always, I give thanks to our Heavenly Father, who never left me in the pit and who breathed life into my dry bones. To Jesus, who died for all my sins and carries every wound I bore turning every pain into purpose. To the Holy Spirit, who strengthens, comforts, convicts, and guides me daily into truth.

To my family who stood with me in my weakest moments, thank you for believing in me even when I struggled to believe in myself. To those who prayed for me, encouraged me, or spoke life into me, your words planted seeds that have now grown into this book.

## About the Author

Maria Davila is a faith-based author, speaker, and missionary who writes from a place of redemption,  resilience, and restored hope. After surviving seasons of rejection, violation, addiction, homelessness, and deep loss, Maria encountered the transforming love of Jesus Christ a love that turned her pain into purpose.

Through her ministry, Healthy Souls International, Inc., she brings practical help and spiritual healing to those in crisis, offering supplies, prayers, and hope to communities recovering from disaster and despair. Her life's mission is to remind every soul that no one is beyond God's reach and that surrender is the doorway to freedom.

Maria is also the author of Homeless Hero: A True Story of Survival, Redemption, and the Power of Faith. It's her testimony of how God can turn brokenness into beauty and use even the darkest moments to reveal His glory.
To learn more about Maria's books, ministry, and upcoming projects, visit: